College and Career Planning

Other titles in the *Money and Finance Guide* series include:

Building a Budget and Savings Plan
Finding a Job and Paying Taxes
Managing Credit and Debt
The Value of Stocks, Bonds, and Investments

Money and Finance Guide

College and Career Planning

Katie John Sharp

ReferencePoint
Press

San Diego, CA

For more information, contact:
ReferencePoint Press, Inc.
PO Box 27779
San Diego, CA 92198
www.ReferencePointPress.com

LIBRARY OF CONGRESS CATALOGING-IN-PUBLICATION DATA

Names: Sharp, Katie John, author.
Title: College and career planning / by Katie Sharp.
Description: San Diego, CA : ReferencePoint Press, Inc., 2021. | Series: Money and finance guide | Includes bibliographical references and index.
Identifiers: LCCN 2020033450 (print) | LCCN 2020033451 (ebook) | ISBN 9781678200527 (library binding) | ISBN 9781678200534 (ebook)
Subjects: LCSH: Vocational guidance--Juvenile literature. | Career development--Juvenile literature. | Occupations--Juvenile literature.
Classification: LCC HF5381 .S5165 2021 (print) | LCC HF5381 (ebook) | DDC 331.702--dc23
LC record available at https://lccn.loc.gov/2020033450
LC ebook record available at https://lccn.loc.gov/2020033451

Contents

What Do You Want to Be When You Grow Up?

How many times have you been asked this question? Probably too many to remember, beginning when you were just a little kid. What would have been your answer when you were four years old? Or ten? The answer you give today may be a lot different. Now that you are in high school and facing important decisions about your future, the question—and your answer—is much more important.

If you are like some people, you have a ready answer. You may have always loved animals and know that you want to be a veterinarian or work at a zoo. Alternatively, your family may have a car repair shop. You may already work there and know that someday you want to run the business yourself. Or you may want to be a teacher, a painter, or a hairdresser. These are all great career options.

What if you have no idea what you want to do? Maybe you don't even know what the possibilities are. Or you are so overwhelmed by the options that you cannot begin to think of an answer, so you're just putting off the decision for another day. That is perfectly normal, too.

Many people have no idea what they want to be when they "grow up." Some people get stuck along the way, and others find a career they didn't expect. Many start out with one career only to change it midway through their lives. The point is that the answer to this question varies, just as it has for you. It's a question that people ask themselves at all ages, even after they are all "grown up."

Your future is waiting. Will it be college, career, or a combination of both?

Whether you know what you want to do after high school or not, it's never too early to start thinking about what comes next. Though you have plenty of time to gather ideas and information, it can be fun to think about the future and the unique ways you can contribute to it.

Chapter One

Eyeing the Future

How well do you know you—what you like and don't like, what you care about, what you are good at and not so great at? Asking yourself these questions can help you make decisions about your future after high school. The better you understand what interests you, what you value, what drives and motivates you, and what you're good at, the more successful you will be at recognizing the job, career, or vocation that will make you happy in your future. Some people at your age are quick to say, "Nothing," "I don't know," "I'll think about it later," or even, "I don't want to think about it!" These questions may sound like the type of thing a nosy parent or friend of the family might ask. However, you might surprise yourself by just how many things you already know, understand, and daydream about doing someday. Just making a start at considering the future may encourage you to think—and focus—on it a bit more.

Getting to Know You

Making lists of what you like and don't like is a good place to start planning your future. Think about the classes, hobbies, and activities you really love or are passionate about. What character traits and skills do they require? What hard skills are required? Math? Curiosity, attention to detail, and analytical skills? Working with your hands?

Taking a closer look at yourself like this is known as a self-assessment. You ask yourself questions. There are no

Deciding your future can seem overwhelming. Start with the basics, make a list of your strengths, weaknesses, and favorite activities.

right or wrong answers. You want to be honest, though, because the answers affect only you. Some of these questions might be a good start:

- **What do you do well?** Think about school subjects as well as other activities. Are you a problem solver? Are you a doodler? Maybe you help your grandparents figure out the remote control or their computer. Clearly, you are not finished with your learning or even knowing what you might excel at, but this gives you a rough idea of your tendencies.
- **What do you do not so well?** It is just as important to recognize subjects and activities you find difficult or frustrating. Perhaps you don't enjoy puzzles or putting

things together. Maybe kids drive you crazy and you are terrified of dogs. Perhaps you're an introvert, and the thought of public speaking gives you a stomachache. All these things may change or soften with experience and practice. And they may not. Make a list of things that turn you off or things you don't think you're good at. Then distinguish between those you don't care to improve and those you would like to do better.

- **What do the people in your life think you're good at?** A different perspective can help you see the talents and abilities that you may not notice about yourself. Conversely, you may find that you reject some of the things others think you are good at. Were there times in your life when someone complimented you and it felt "right"? When you did a good job and you knew that person was giving you an honest opinion—these are good "moments" to remember when assessing your strengths.

- **What job(s) do you have or have you had? What do or did you like and dislike about the job(s)?** Do you enjoy working with people? Do you like to clean or fix things? Do you like to be in charge or simply follow orders? Make a list of your job responsibilities. Then rate each one; do you like or dislike that chore? Do you excel at or need to work on it?

- **What do you enjoy doing in your free time?** The kind of activities you do for fun can be clues to the skills you are good at and enjoy.

- **Whom do you admire or look up to?** These people can tell you about values and characteristics that are important to you. They may also be examples of careers you would like to investigate.

- **Do you enjoy learning, studying, and going to school?** Some careers take several years of education, while others are learned on the job or with just a few more years of schooling.

If you want to dig deeper into what "makes you tick," you can find more self-assessment tools online. These sites make self-assessment fun and easy. For example, CareerShip (see For Further Research on p. 70) is an "online career exploration adventure." According to its website, it is "a free online exploration adventure for middle and high school students."[1]

Some people have an idea about what they want to do but may not be set on a specific career. Or they may know what interests them but not be sure how that translates into a job—that's okay. Life experiences and exposure will reveal the careers that fit. Gabe, a high school student, is interested in social work. "At least that's the most formal way of describing it," he says. "So long as I am helping people, I suppose it doesn't matter exactly what I'm doing."[2] Other students have very specific career goals in mind, and even have "dream jobs." Another current high school student, Emily, wants to be "a foreign diplomat for the U.S. State Department. My dream job would be Secretary of State, but that is very much a dream job."[3]

Exploring Careers

As you think about your life after high school, you do not need to choose *the* job or career you will do for the rest of your life. That is nearly impossible. Most people change their minds several times as their interests and the world change. Think about how quickly technology changes. Not that long ago, careers in social media didn't even exist—because there was no social media. But with growing and changing technology and social media platforms, those careers are now booming. And as comedian Stephen Colbert once said in a commencement speech, "Thankfully, dreams can change. If we'd all stuck with our first dream, the world would be overrun with princesses and cowboys."[4]

"Thankfully, dreams can change. If we'd all stuck with our first dream, the world would be overrun with princesses and cowboys."[4]

—Stephen Colbert, comedian

The Top Careers of 2020

You live in a time when jobs and careers are ever evolving. When your grandparents or parents were graduating from high school, there were no jobs in social media or website development. There were no podcast producers or app developers. Chances are, some of the jobs your grandparents did no longer exist today. And the job you might have in the future may not even exist yet; you might be the first in your field!

There are also certain jobs that will never change, such as those in accounting, medicine, and education. The techniques and technology students learn and professionals use in these fields may change, but the basic job descriptions will remain pretty much the same.

According to *U.S. News & World Report*, using data from the Bureau of Labor Statistics, these were some of the top jobs in 2020. The criteria that put them at the top include average income, work-life balance, and expected job growth. Do any of these jobs appeal to you?

Database administrator	Physician
Dentist	Physician assistant
Financial advisor	Software developer
IT manager	Speech-language pathologist
Nurse practitioner	Statistician
Oral surgeon	Veterinarian
Orthodontist	Web developer

While you don't need to make a final career choice right now, it is a good idea to know your options and think about what you want to do after high school. This can help set you on the right path to eventually landing in the place that's right for you.

Carl, who recently received his PhD in analytical chemistry, knew what he wanted to do while he was still in high school. "I decided [what I wanted to be] during the second semester of my senior year in high school. . . . I excelled in my chemistry and physics courses in high school and had an excellent teacher. That had much to do with my decision. Plus, I always like mixing things together and measuring things."[5] Carl knew his strengths and interests and was able to make a successful career out of them. Not everyone figures all of this out in high school, and that's perfectly normal.

Listing the Possibilities

Start your research by making a list of careers, jobs, and/or opportunities that sound interesting to you. If you need help getting started, there are ways to discover options. For example, ask the adults in your life about their job or career. Talk to your parents, guardian, grandparents, aunts, and uncles. Ask your parents' friends, or your friend's parents. Most people love to talk about what they do. If you are intrigued by what you learn from someone in particular, ask if you can shadow him or her at work. This is a great way to see how people, from construction workers to naturalists to hospital administrators, spend their time at work each day.

You also can find out about careers and other opportunities online. Enter the word "careers" in a search engine, and you will get back many hits. Be sure to look for trustworthy sites. You can also go directly to job and career websites. For example, the Bureau of Labor Statistics (see Websites on p. 72) keeps track of facts about careers of the past, present, and future. The site even has a page specifically designed for students who want to explore careers. The page offers several resources to students, including a career outlook page, where you can search specific careers.

For example, if you search "social media specialists," you'll find out what they do, how to become one, and what to expect in that role. This information can help you decide if your interests, skills, and life goals match various careers.

Another way to discover jobs is to observe people working. When you enter a school, store, restaurant, doctor's office, park, or community center, take notice of the people who work there. What are they doing? If their work looks interesting to you, talk to them about it. Ask if they'd be willing to answer your questions. You can find out what they do, how they trained for the job, and what they would suggest you do to find out more.

Finally, talk to your school guidance counselor. He or she likely knows past graduates and others who do jobs that might interest you. Your counselor can help you network with these people. He

Talking to your school counselor or an adult you respect can help you decide your first steps toward a career.

or she also probably has access to resources, both print and on-line, to help you explore careers. Your counselor has likely helped many students make decisions about their future. Those students (who are now in college or working in a career) can serve as great resources to help you learn about jobs and careers.

With these resources and more, you should be able to complete a list of ten or so careers that look interesting enough to you to research further.

Making a Connection

Once you have a list of jobs, careers, and other opportunities, you can learn more about each one. Here are some questions you might want to consider:

- What characteristics are needed to do the job?
- What skills are required? What other skills would help?
- How much and what kind of schooling is required?
- Is the job in high demand? Will it be easy to find a job?
- What does the job pay?
- Is the job specific to certain parts of the country or the world?

Your goal is to match what you learn about yourself from do-ing a self-assessment with the jobs, careers, and other opportu-nities you discover through your research. For example, if you find you're really interested in the health care field but the thought of blood makes you queasy, then perhaps being a doctor or nurse isn't the right path. That doesn't mean health care is out of the question, though. There are other opportunities in this field, in-cluding occupational therapy, pharmacy, medical coding, ultra-sound technology, and more.

Christy, who now works as a teacher, wishes she had spent more time exploring careers in high school. "I don't think I had a counselor or that 'person' introduce me to what skills I have and what I would be good at using those skills. I went to a large

More Ways to Explore Careers

You can find out more jobs and careers that interest you in many different ways. You just need to look for opportunities and take advantage of them.

Get involved: Explore your interests by joining groups, both inside and outside of school. Work on the yearbook, try out for a sport, or join the drama club at school or the choir at your place of worship. Find groups that already exist or start a new one. Chances are there are others who have the same interests as you.

Take classes: Look for classes you can take in your community, such as art or music classes with a local artist. Summer is always a good time to learn a new talent or skill that might spark a career interest. Your local community center or place of worship may offer some classes, as well.

Jobs and internships: Experiencing a job firsthand is one of the best ways to learn new skills and get experience in a workplace environment. You can learn about what you do and do not want to do in the future this way. For example, you may learn that you will never be happy sitting in an office cubicle day in and day out. You may realize that you want to work with your hands, build something, or work in nature. To find job openings, check local websites and community boards or talk to your guidance counselor. Camps, restaurants, and retail stores often need part-time help.

Internships can be a great introduction to your field of choice.

suburban high school, and I felt like a number. [If I could do it again], I would reach out to counselors or career centers and really investigate choices to see what's out there."[6]

If you learn about a career that piques your interest, find ways to learn more about it. For example, look for opportunities to volunteer. If you think you want to work with animals, local animal shelters may need volunteers to walk dogs and clean cages. If you want to work in health care, try volunteering at a hospital. Visit websites to find volunteer opportunities near you. You can also ask adults, including your guidance counselor, for ideas.

One of the best ways to find out more about a career that interests you is to seek out people who currently work in that field. Talk to the adults in your life to see whether they can introduce you to people they know who can help. Set up a time to talk with people about what they do, how they got their job, what they do each day, and how they trained for and got the job. Ask them what they love about their job and what parts of the job aren't that great.

With all this research, hopefully you will have an idea or two about what you might want to do after high school graduation. The next step is to figure out what to do next.

Chapter Two

College Bound

If you've decided that college is your next step, there are more decisions to make. Deciding which college to attend and how to pay for it can be overwhelming—especially when so many people quiz you on your progress. "It seemed everywhere I went, people asked me, 'What did you get on the SAT?' 'How did you do?' 'Have you applied to college?' 'What college are planning to attend?' 'Where are you going?' 'What schools did you get accepted to?'"[7] says Katherine Schwarzenegger in her book *I Just Graduated . . . Now What?* While the people in your life mean well, their questions may instead stress you out.

Don't allow anxiety to get the best of you. Try to take things one step at a time.

College Considerations

Going to college can be a great way to learn and practice the skills required to work in a specific field such as teaching, banking, or health care. For many careers, college is a redundant prerequisite, and others require a stint in graduate school. Many students attend college with one course of study, or major, in mind and end up changing their minds—sometimes several times. There is no doubt that college is a learning experience in many different ways.

For students who aren't quite sure what they want to study, college can be a way to meet new people and explore options. Students can try different classes and experiences in search of something that "clicks." This type of exploration comes with a hefty price tag, however. If you truly have no idea what you want to study, you might think about attending a community college, which is much less expensive. Community colleges offer a variety of classes that allow you to explore different fields.

College offers a lot more than "job training," however. If you attend a college away from home, it's a way to learn how to take care of yourself and be independent. It's also a place to meet people, get involved with causes that are important to you, and learn about the world, other cultures, and experiences.

College is a great way to meet new people and discover new walks of life.

Traditionally, students move away from home to attend college. They often live in a dorm and take classes, meet new friends, and learn about life away from their families, all with the goal of getting a degree that will eventually lead to a career. These days, however, college looks a lot different for many students. While quite a few still follow the traditional model, others take classes online, study abroad, or complete internships.

Types of Colleges

Students considering college have several choices. Among them are two-year and four-year colleges and universities, public and private schools, and more. Finding a college that fits you is a first step in exploring your options. Choosing the right college may be a piece of cake for some and an impossible decision for others.

Two-Year Colleges

Two-year colleges include community colleges, technical colleges, and junior colleges and can be private or public. Students who attend a two-year college work toward an associate's degree. They also may earn a certificate. They may graduate and work as a computer support technician, paralegal, farm manager, child care worker, graphic designer, and more. Other students may transfer to a four-year program to continue their studies.

More and more students are choosing to attend two-year colleges. Many simply can't afford to get a four-year degree, especially when they don't have a good handle on what they want to study. Students who go to community college can save money in several ways. For one, the cost of a two-year college is less than a four-year college. In two years, students can earn an associate's degree that can lead to great job opportunities. According to Education USA, "Community colleges often lead the United States in educating students in cutting-edge fields such as biomedical technology, biotechnology, robotics, laser optics, internet and computer technologies, and geographic information systems."[8] Taking this route to the workplace can be a huge cost savings. Combine it with living at home, and the savings grow.

What's more, attending a two-year college is a great way to explore careers to find out what really interests you while not spending a lot of money. Community colleges, for example, offer classes in different fields, from child care to health care, accounting, sociology, and photography. Once you find something that seems interesting, there are several options to prepare you for a career in that field. For example, you can remain at the two-year college, get an associate's degree, and move into the workforce. Or, after taking a few classes, you can move on to a four-year college to get a bachelor's degree and beyond. You can even stay at the two-year college to knock out general education classes that any four-year college will require. Taking these classes at a community college costs far less than it would at a four-year school.

A two-year college also makes sense if your grade point average (GPA) from high school needs a boost. Four-year colleges have become harder to get into, thanks to increased competition and tougher requirements. Attending a two-year college can give you a chance to work on your GPA—but make no mistake, you still need to put in the work. Classes at two-year colleges are tough, but you can take a couple at a time, helping you concentrate your efforts and achieve better grades. Once you have completed a few classes, you can apply to a four-year college.

Finally, community colleges allow students to go to school part-time while working a part-time job to help pay expenses. This flexibility may be the only way some students can afford college. Whichever path you take, a two-year college can help you shape your future while saving you money.

Four-Year Schools

The terms *university* and *college*, in the United States at least, generally refer to post-secondary education. Universities comprise a number of different colleges on one campus, such as a college of liberal arts, a college of engineering, a college of education, and so on, and offer advanced degrees in addition to bachelor degrees.

College Degrees Lead to Better Jobs

As the job market continues to become more dependent on technical skill sets, those with a college education continue to earn more money. This graph shows that income levels for those who earned bachelor's degrees increased significantly from 1991 to 2016, while incomes for those with less education actually went down.

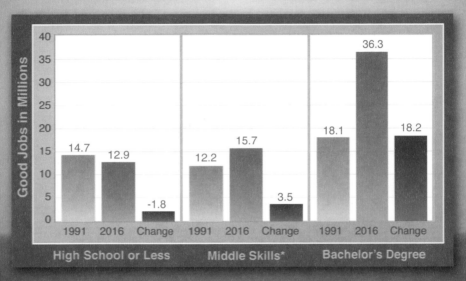

*The information above is based on jobs that pay between $35,000 and $65,000 per year. *Middle skills* is defined as having more education than a high school diploma, but less than a bachelor's degree.

Source: Center on Education and the Workforce, 3300 Whitehaven St. NW, Suite 3200, Washington, DC 20007. https://cew.georgetown.edu.

Undergraduates at four-year schools work toward a bachelor of science or bachelor of arts degree. Graduates may decide to enter the workforce or continue their education by working toward a master's degree or doctorate.

Each college within a university offers classes in an area of study, such as business, engineering, education, or liberal arts. Most state-run or highly reputed universities have a large and diverse student body and often have large, sprawling campuses. Because they are so large, universities offer students many opportunities for rounding out their education with activities such as athletic programs, fraternities and sororities, various student organizations, and more.

Students considering a large university have to be comfortable learning in classes with a lot of other students and without a lot of one-on-one guidance or attention. In general, the lower-

A four-year college can open more doors for exciting careers and increased earning potential.

level classes are quite big, with maybe hundreds of students. As students enroll in courses specific to their major, the classes become more focused and smaller. Students who attend big schools want choices, both socially and academically, but need to be able to focus on their studies amid the hustle and bustle of a busy campus.

Students who prefer a smaller, more intimate experience may consider a small college. Not only is the student body smaller, but the campuses are, too. Some of these colleges are referred to as "liberal arts colleges." These schools give students an education in a broad, or liberal, range of academic areas, including arts, sciences, and humanities.

Universities can be public or private, and they can be quite expensive. However, students have many opportunities to seek financial aid in the form of loans, grants, and scholarships. Students who go to a state-run university in their home state generally pay less tuition than students who go to a private university or a university out of state.

Narrowing Your List

When you've decided you're going to college, start listing schools to consider. With so many choices, several schools will be a great fit for you. You just need to find a school where you feel you will thrive and that will meet your budget, wants, and needs. In a *Forbes* opinion piece, Chad Orzel, who writes about science, offers this insight:

> Ultimately, education isn't something a college or university does *to you*, it's something *you do for yourself*. Colleges and universities are in the business of providing resources for students to use in shaping their own education. . . . In the end they are all just tools that students will use to fashion their future. . . . You can find the necessary resources to get a quality education just about anywhere.[9]

As you add colleges to your list, keep in mind certain criteria, such as the following:

- **Size.** If a big school with tens of thousands of students is not for you, then you've narrowed your choices to medium-size to small schools.
- **Location.** Do you want to be close to home or as far away as possible?
- **Reputation.** If you know what you want to study, you'll want to find schools that have strong programs in that field. If you aren't sure just yet, make sure the school in general meets certain academic criteria.
- **Finances.** Schools often offer scholarships and grants, and there are other forms of financial aid and loans for students in need. How much financial help a certain school can offer you can be a determining factor in your choice.
- **Extracurricular activities.** If you want to go to football games, join a fraternity or sorority, be involved in groups such as Model UN, or play in an orchestra, for example, choose schools that offer activities you are interested in.

College choices are personal, and you need to do your research and figure out what criteria are most important to you. Fortunately, thanks to the internet, such research isn't that difficult. Several resources are available to help you find schools that meet your needs and wants. For example, your school guidance counselor is a great resource. He or she has helped many other students discover and choose schools. He or she likely communicates with schools around the country and beyond and knows a lot about different schools you may have never heard of.

When choosing a college, Sophie, a current college student, advises, "If you're looking at a school in a different region of the

United States than the one you live in, know that it's going to be a long adjustment, and take that into consideration. Look at several different programs at the school to make sure that if you want to switch majors, you'll be able to."[10] Navid, a recent college graduate now working in advertising, suggests:

"Think holistically. The majority of the experience I gained in college was outside of the classroom, so consider the campus size, groups you want to be involved in, and where you feel most comfortable."[11]

—Navid, recent college graduate

Think holistically. The majority of the experience I gained in college was outside of the classroom, so consider the campus size, groups you want to be involved in, and where you feel most comfortable. I passed up on a full-ride scholarship to a larger state school because I felt that I would have a better experience at a smaller university, and even though it cost me more money at the time, it proved to be well worth it in the long run.[11]

Emily, a recent four-year college graduate, shares this advice about choosing a college: "Definitely look into colleges' traditions and campus life. While academics and money are important, you do still want to have that sense of community that college is supposed to bring, so making sure the schools you're applying to have those traditions to create that community should be on your list of things to research."[12] And Myla, who just graduated from high school, shares, "They are several reasons why I chose my school. . . . [My school] has great ethnic diversity. I have my own dorm

"Definitely look into colleges' traditions and campus life. While academics and money are important, you do still want to have that sense of community that college is supposed to bring, so making sure the schools you're applying to have those traditions to create that community should be on your list of things to research."[12]

—Emily, current college student

room, and I am able to have my car on campus. . . . In addition, I will graduate college with no student loan debt."[13]

When investigating schools, the internet is your best resource. For example, if you want to study creative writing, search "best colleges for creative writing," and see what comes up. Visit schools' websites to learn more about them. As you find schools that meet your criteria, write them down. Then spend more time researching each school and deciding whether you want to apply.

College fairs are another way to find out about schools. Representatives from several schools come to college fairs to share information and can answer questions. Your guidance counselor should be able to help you locate college fairs near you. Sometimes college representatives also visit high schools.

Before applying to schools, narrow down your choices. You will have to pay a fee to apply to each school. With some imagination and assertiveness, however, you may be able to avoid some application fees. For example, in 2020 SaVion Smith, a high school student from College Park, Georgia, announced he had been accepted to thirty-two colleges. That means he filled out a lot of college applications! Smith says he went to a lot of college fairs and applied there to keep the application costs down. Kayla Willis, a student from South Fulton, Georgia, also received several acceptance letters—at least thirty-one. She, too, avoided the application fees. Willis asked schools to waive the fee and only applied to those schools that agreed to do so.

You can narrow your college choices by doing some additional research into schools on your list. Peruse websites, talk to college representatives, engage students who currently attend the schools, reach out to graduates, read reviews, and so on. For those schools that pass your tests, plan a campus visit. There is no better way to get a feel for a campus, the students, and the general environment of a school than to walk its

Community College Considerations

Aside from the savings, two-year programs offer several other advantages, depending on the reasons and goals for attending college. For one, these programs are often flexible in terms of how to take classes. For example many offer online classes. Students can listen to lectures and participate in classes from just about anywhere.

Another advantage is the teachers and professors. According to the US Department of Education, teachers in associate's degree programs spend more time than teachers at other types of colleges conducting demonstrations and leading practical exercises. Many of these instructors work in the field in which they teach. This means they are able to relate firsthand stories and experiences of life on the job.

Statistics show that people who graduate with an associate's degree earn more and are more likely to find jobs than high school graduates who do not continue their education. And according to Bryan, an avionics technician who graduated from a technical school:

> Two benefits of technical school are the lower cost of tuition and help with job placement, which is usually quite rigorous. The opportunities in technical and trade schools are specialized, making graduates great assets [to] the companies that hire them; plumbers, welders, and heavy machine operators start out making high salaries, especially if they are hired by union-run companies. Compared to four-year colleges, you can learn a marketable skill in a shorter amount of time and begin a career making a living wage sooner without the huge student loan debt.

Bryan, interview with the author, June 10, 2020.

grounds and buildings. Sera, who now works for a tech company, explains how she narrowed her choices, "I visited different types of schools and determined that I liked small schools best. I ended up visiting and choosing a small liberal arts school because I had read about it in a book called *Colleges That Change Lives* and it offered a lot of things I was looking for."[14]

Riley, a current college student, says she "mostly looked at where my school was in academic rankings for my chosen area of study. I knew I didn't have good enough grades or enough money to go to a school that was well recognized, but I still wanted to learn from the best that I could."[15]

Applying to College

College experts recommend students begin applying to schools by the beginning of their senior year. Each college has its own deadline, so it's important to keep track of those. Some high school guidance counselors advise students to finish their applications by Halloween so they can relax and enjoy the rest of their senior year. On the *U.S. News & World Report*'s Education web page, Christine Chu, a college admissions counselor, suggests making a to-do list to get through applications. "Once you can see it visually, the number of tasks and a schedule to do them, it simplifies a lot of things," she says. "It will take away a lot of the anxiety."[16]

Essays and Letters

Most applications have certain requirements you can address first. These include writing a college essay and securing letters of recommendation. Your counselor or a teacher can give you tips for writing your essay. There are also books and websites that offer guidance.

For the letters of recommendation, ask two people (not relatives) who know you well: teachers, coaches, bosses, volunteer supervisors, spiritual leaders, and so on. Choose people with whom you have a good relationship and who will effectively communicate your best qualities. Ask early, because some people, teachers especially, get a lot of requests and need time.

The Common Application

Today hundreds of schools accept the Common Application. The beauty of this application is that you fill it out once and can submit it to multiple colleges. Be aware, however, that some schools have a supplemental section that may include additional questions. Some schools will not accept the Common Application, however. They may accept similar application platforms, such as the Coalition Application, the Universal College Application, and others. Visit each school's website to find out which applications it will accept.

Most applications will also require the following:

- **Transcripts.** Schools will want a current transcript as well as your final transcript after you finish high school.
- **Standardized test scores.** These include the SAT and/or ACT. Not all schools require these, however. Check the requirements for each school to which you apply.
- **Résumé.** A résumé is a list of the things you have done through high school, aside from taking classes. This includes volunteer work, jobs, sports, leadership roles, clubs, and more. Colleges generally like applicants who are well rounded and have a variety of interests. It's a good idea to get involved in activities as early as possible so you can add them to this list. Even if you aren't the type to get involved, there are likely things you do that you can include to "beef up" your résumé.
- **Portfolio/auditions.** Some schools may require a portfolio, depending on the field you hope to study. Art majors, for example, may need to show examples of their work. Music majors may need to audition to show their talent.

Each school will make it clear what is required to complete an application for admission. As mentioned earlier, make a to-do list. Better yet, make a to-do list for each school you're applying to so that you are sure to submit everything that's required.

You're In! Now What?

Congratulations! You've been accepted to one or more schools. Now you have to decide which one you'll attend. You'll have to consider the cost and what you can afford. College is expensive, and you have to expect some cost for a good education, but you don't want to spend too much money or put yourself into too much debt. A hefty loan payment after graduation can put a lot of pressure on you to find a job that will pay you enough to live *and* pay off that debt.

When colleges send acceptance letters, they communicate the costs and any financial aid they are willing to offer. Most colleges will help at least a little bit—they do want you to attend, after all. They may offer scholarships or grants—money you don't have to pay back. They may offer you a job on campus, called work study. They might offer you loans, too—money you do have to pay back. A good way to compare college costs is to create a spreadsheet that includes the total cost of each college—including tuition, fees, room and board, books and supplies, travel home for breaks and holidays, and other living expenses—and the amount of money you have to spend—including your savings, money your parents or other relatives are willing to contribute, and money the college has offered. You can also use free online tools and college planning calculators designed to help you compare college costs. The Consumer Financial Protection Bureau offers a free tool on its website that allows users to easily compare college costs and financial aid among three schools at a time. Users visit www .consumerfinance.gov/paying-for-college/compare-financial -aid-and-college-cost, fill in the name of up to three schools,

There are many opportunities for scholarships and financial aid; make sure you explore all options.

and answer a few questions. The site then reveals a side-by-side comparison of the schools' costs and other financial information based on the student's responses.

The next step is to see whether there are other sources of money to tap into. You may be able to secure scholarships. Local organizations in your hometown might offer scholarships to high school seniors. Your guidance counselor will likely know about these opportunities. Also, check websites that list scholarships available to students nationwide. You may be amazed to see the number of groups and organizations that want to give money to aspiring college students. However, these scholarships aren't handouts awarded to just anyone who asks. You often have to prove you deserve the money, and you may have to belong to a certain ethnic group or have a relative in a certain social or other organization.

One of the best ways to secure funds for college is federal and state financial aid. Most colleges require you to fill out the

Is College Worth It?

Many students begin life after college owing a lot of money. These factors have to make a student wonder: is college worth it? The answer is highly personal. Each person has to make this decision for him- or herself based on his or her life goals and values.

According to the Bureau of Labor Statistics, college is still a good idea in terms of making money after graduation. As the bureau looks at it, "The more you learn, the more you earn." In October 2019, 76 percent of twenty- to twenty-nine-year-olds who received a bachelor's degree in 2019 had secured a job.

However, in 2020 an article in the *Washington Post* cited a report that painted a different picture. According to the report, "Our results suggest that college and postgraduate education may be failing some recent graduates as a financial investment. . . . The wealth-building advantage of higher education has declined among recent graduates of all demographic groups."

Regardless, many students still feel it's a good idea to go to college. Indeed, two out of three high school graduates ages sixteen to twenty-four were enrolled in colleges and universities in 2019.

Elka Torpey, "Measuring the Value of an Education," Bureau of Labor Statistics, 2018. www.bls.gov.

Quoted in Michelle Singletary, "Is College Still Worth It? Read This Study," *Washington Post*, January 11, 2020. www.washingtonpost.com.

Free Application for Federal Student Aid. You can find the application online at www.fafsa.ed.gov. To complete the application, you need to list the schools you might attend and include your family's income information. Plus, all male students must register for selective service on their eighteenth birthday. Shortly after completing and processing the application, you will receive a Student Aid Report, which tells you what aid you can expect and how much you're expected to pay. This is an estimate, but it will help you decide which schools you can afford.

You will find that there are other ways to help pay your tuition and other bills. You can work while taking classes. Many students work at restaurants or as babysitters or tutors, for example. If you go to a school close to home, you can save money by living at home, if that's possible. Madi, now a graphic designer, attended a private school. Tuition, room and board, and fees added up to well over $40,000 a year—a price she could not afford. However, almost half that cost was for room and board. She decided to live at home and commute to campus each day. Because she also had saved money while in high school and received scholarships and federal aid, she was able to pay tuition without taking out any loans. She graduated from college in four years debt-free. "I missed out on much of the traditional college experience of living in a dorm and hanging out with friends on campus, but in the end it was worth it to me,"[17] Madi says.

You can always find ways to cut corners with college costs. For example, you don't need to go to the most expensive school just because your best friend goes there. You don't need to live in the fanciest dorm. Use your imagination to find ways to chip away at that final cost. Your future self will thank you for it. After all, college is a time for sacrifice. The goal is to get an education so you can move on to a good a job after graduation. It should not break you or your family financially. One way to look at it is this: live like a college student while you're in school so you don't have to live like a college student for the rest of your life.

Cost is definitely a big part of your decision about which college to attend. But it isn't the only thing that matters. When it comes to making your final decision, you need to weigh your career goals, your educational wants and needs, and what you can afford.

Chapter Three

Alternatives to Traditional College

If you want to continue your education after high school, traditional college is not the only way. You may know your passion doesn't require a bachelor's degree. You may be ready to put the structure of traditional school and learning behind you. Maybe you learn better in alternative ways. Or perhaps you simply can't afford the high cost of college—and if you know college is not for you, why spend that money just to prove it? Does that mean you can't be successful in a career? Absolutely not. You can still get an education that will lead to a successful career.

"Life after high school is definitely harder," says Lia, a college graduate, "but putting the time and the work in whether you're in the workforce, military, or college, is so rewarding. You will make mistakes along the way, but as long as you can learn from them, they will make you better off in the end."[18] And Bill, also a college graduate, adds:

> "Life after high school is definitely harder, but putting the time and the work in whether you're in the workforce, military, or college, is so rewarding. You will make mistakes along the way, but as long as you can learn from them, they will make you better off in the end."[18]
>
> —Lia, college graduate

Don't limit yourself, and don't feel like college is the only way. If it is for you, great. But, don't be afraid to change your mind, either about your major or about staying at all. Figure [out] what you really want to do. The rest of your life, if you're lucky, is a long time. You might as well enjoy it, and do something that doesn't make you dread the alarm clock. Even better: Do something that makes you so excited that you don't need one.[19]

Online Classes

Today you no longer have to sit in a classroom to get a good education. Now you can learn while sitting at home, at a library, or even in a coffee shop. You just need a computer and an internet connection. In fact, more students are choosing to take online classes. According to the National Center for Education Statistics, in the fall of 2018 more than 3 million students were enrolled exclusively in online programs, and most of those students were undergraduates.

Online learning offers many advantages. At the top of the list is flexibility. You can take classes on your own schedule and at your own pace. You can work part-time or full-time and take classes. What's more, you can work on a degree from just about any school in the world, from the comfort of your own home. You do need to be careful, however, that the school you choose is reputable. You want to be sure it is accredited, which means it meets minimum standards and adheres to certain goals and standards recognized as important to a quality education.

"Don't limit yourself, and don't feel like college is the only way. If it is for you, great. But, don't be afraid to change your mind, either about your major or about staying at all. Figure out what you really want to do . . . and do something that doesn't make you dread the alarm clock. Even better: Do something that makes you so excited that you don't need one."[19]

—Bill, college graduate

Online schools can be expensive, and some can be scams. Be sure to speak with a school representative directly for information about the school and its costs before enrolling. It's also a good idea to talk with people who have attended the school or seek out testimonials online that you can verify are true.

Do You Need a Degree to Get a Job?

As proof that you can have a successful career without a traditional college degree, below are some jobs that don't require a bachelor's or advanced degree. Training is required for some of these jobs, including perhaps an associate's degree or certificate, but you don't need to graduate from a four-year college. For some, all you need is a high school diploma and some work experience.

According to the Bureau of Labor Statistics, several occupations that require less than a bachelor's degree pay above the nation's median salary of $37,690. While workers with a degree often make more money than those without a degree, good-paying jobs are out there for those who cannot go or choose not to go to a four-year college.

The following jobs do not require a formal education above a high school diploma. Listed on the *U.S. News & World Report* website, these jobs, according to the U.S. Bureau of Labor Statistics, have the largest projected number and percentage of openings from 2018 to 2028:

Home health aide	Massage therapist
Medical assistant	Dental assistant
Medical records technician	Solar photovoltaic installer
Landscaper and groundskeeper	Physical therapist aide
Personal care aide	Nail technician

U.S. News & World Report, "How U.S. News Ranks the Best Jobs," January 7, 2020. https://money.usnews.com.

Free (or Low-Cost) Online Classes

Believe it or not, you can take some online classes at little or no cost. In fact, there are quite a few options. Massive open on-line courses (MOOCs) are offered by companies in partnership with colleges and universities. Companies that offer such classes include edX, Coursera, and more. Granted, these are not your typical classes with a live instructor; they are more often pre-recorded lectures that students can watch anytime, anywhere. As these classes have grown in popularity, more companies are offering added options such as feedback from an instructor and certificates of completion—for an extra fee. Even when there is a cost, however, these classes are still a lot cheaper than attending a traditional college program.

MOOCs are a great opportunity for people to learn certain skills, but they take self-discipline, since no one is checking in on you and motivating you to "attend" and keep up. Many partici-pants take these classes to learn skills that may help them get a job or help them move up in a current job. MOOCs are also popular among people who want to start their own businesses. Students who are already working toward a degree might find that free online classes help them dig deeper into topics that in-terest them.

Learning a Skill or Trade

Another option if traditional college is not for you is to learn a skill or trade that will help you get a job. Schools that train students in such skills go by different names: trade school, vocational school, career college, and technical college. Whatever you call them, these schools offer a degree, diploma, or certificate in a wide variety of fields, including information technology, engineering, agriculture, business administration, culinary arts, cosmetology, construction, and health care. Some jobs that people secure after completing such a program include dental hygienist, electrician, plumber, chef, and beautician.

At one time, the trades were considered to be good, honorable jobs, and many high schools offered classes like shop to help introduce students to these career options. However, according to Matthew B. Crawford, author of *Shop Class as Soulcraft*:

> High-school shop-class programs were widely dismantled in the 1990s as educators prepared students to become "knowledge workers." The imperative of the last 20 years to round up every warm body and send it to college, then to the cubicle, was tied to a vision of the future in which we somehow take leave of material reality and glide about in a pure information economy. This has not come to pass. . . . Now as ever, somebody has to actually do things: fix our cars, unclog our toilets, build our houses.[20]

"The imperative of the last 20 years to round up every warm body and send it to college, then to the cubicle, was tied to a vision of the future in which we somehow take leave of material reality and glide about in a pure information economy. This has not come to pass. . . . Now as ever, somebody has to actually do things: fix our cars, unclog our toilets, build our houses."[20]

—Matthew B. Crawford, author, *Shop Class as Soulcraft*

No doubt, many jobs involve relatively new technology, but people still need workers who will do jobs considered "trades." The trades include plumbers, car mechanics, electricians, and heating, ventilating, and air-conditioning (HVAC) technicians. Crawford points out that while technology-based jobs can and often are sent to other countries, such as China, the more hands-on trades will never be shipped overseas. A car mechanic has to have his or her hands on the car in order to repair it. And people will always need their car, plumbing, heating, and so on fixed. This means there will always be a need for trade workers.

Trade schools are a great option for hands-on-type people. Not everyone is college-bound, and that's okay.

There are ways to learn a trade other than in school, but trade school has its advantages. Trade schools typically do not require general education courses—think English, biology, or history—to graduate. Instead, the focus is on courses that train students to do a job. Students get hands-on training in their field and may do internships, gaining experience working with professionals in the field in a real-life work environment. Trade schools are especially good for people who learn better by *doing* instead of solely by reading textbooks and listening to lectures.

Most students can complete a trade school program in two years or less, but some programs can take up to four years. Students who finish earn a certificate, diploma, or associate's degree.

When the time comes to choose a school, be sure the school is legitimate. Read testimonials and/or seek out graduates and ask them for feedback on their experience. Make sure the schools you apply to are accredited, or meet certain criteria, so you know employers will feel confident that you've been trained according to industry standards.

Before you plunk down money for trade school, find out if it's even necessary to complete such a program to get an entry-level job in the field you want to work. You may not need to spend the time and money. Your guidance counselor or someone who works in the field should be able to tell you. If you decide trade school is the right path, ask each school you're considering whether its graduates are earn a licensure or certification after they complete the program. You also can check websites to find information about the skills and training you need for a particular job. Two such websites are O*NET OnLine (www.onetonline.org) and CareerOneStop (www.careeronestop.org).

Another consideration is cost. For each school you consider, request the total cost of the program. Find out whether there any costs not included in the total price, such as books, supplies, equipment, fees, and the like. These schools sometimes come with a hefty price tag, so if you'll need help paying, ask about financial aid.

When you've decided on a program, you may have to sign a contract upon enrollment. In it, you agree to pay the costs in exchange for an education. Be sure the contract lists how much the program will cost, how long it will last, and the refund policy. Read the entire document—ask an adult for assistance to be safe—and do not sign it until all your questions are answered.

Consider a Trade

As Matthew B. Crawford points out in his book *Shop Class as Soulcraft*, for years there was a push to get high school graduates to go to college, graduate, and take a desk job. These "white-collar" jobs typically were seen as the goal of any forward-thinking student. So-called blue-collar jobs typically were seen as less desirable, something people who aren't as smart or successful had to settle for.

But with the increasing cost of college, trade jobs—including those in construction, plumbing, HVAC installation and repair, and more—are growing in demand. Not only is there a tremendous need for these workers, the benefits of getting into these occupations are many. Training for these jobs is much less expensive than a four-year college, and the pay and benefits can be impressive too. According to the Bureau of Labor Statistics, construction jobs are expected to grow by 10 percent through 2028. That's faster than any other occupation. These jobs include those for electricians, boilermakers, roofers, ironworkers, carpenters, and inspectors.

When you look into training for such jobs, thoroughly check the credentials of the institution before you sign papers or pay any money. Make sure the programs it provides are accredited. It's also a good idea to be sure the school helps with job placement. If you don't mind getting your hands dirty and you like to build things, solve problems, and work hard, a job in the trades may be right up your alley.

Many jobs can bring satisfaction, challenge, and happiness. Find what works for you.

Joining the Military

Some students consider joining the military after high school graduation. There are several benefits to doing so, including making money for college, being able to travel the world, feeling a sense of purpose in serving your country, and getting technical training.

There are five branches of the military: army, air force, navy, marine corps, and coast guard. If you are considering the mili-

Career fairs at school are a great way to find out more information about a career in the military.

tary, read up on each branch—even if you think you know which one you'd like to join. Each one is different, with different requirements, commitments, and benefits. Read testimonials or find people who have served or are currently serving. Ask them what it's like and why they joined. You can also visit each branch's website and request information. As you compare the branches, consider several factors, including length of enlistment, pay, length and type of training, enlistment bonuses, and ability to pursue higher education.

If you have decided to enlist, the next step is to take the Armed Services Vocational Aptitude Battery. This is an aptitude test that the military uses to determine the qualifications of candidates for enlistment. It also helps in placing enlistees in military occupational programs.

Chapter Four

Careers Without College

Don't ever let someone tell you that you can't have a career without a college degree. Many careers don't require a degree. For example, many people who forgo college start their own businesses. They see a need and fulfill it, or they have an entrepreneurial spirit and the know-how to use it. Blake Mycoskie, the founder of TOMS shoes, went to college, but he didn't stay for long. In Katherine Schwarzenegger's book, *I Just Graduated . . . Now What?*, he shares:

> "I don't think college is for everyone. School is awesome, but for me I was learning a lot more outside the classroom in the real world than when I was in school."[21]
>
> —Blake Mycoskie, founder of TOMS shoes

While attending SMU [Southern Methodist University] at age nineteen, I started my first company. It was a door-to-door laundry business called EZ Laundry that really took off. Eventually I was so busy doing other people's laundry that I didn't have time to go to school. I fell in love with the entrepreneurial experience and decided to focus my time on business instead of studying. I don't think college is for everyone. School is awesome, but for me I was learning a lot more outside the classroom in the real world than when I was in school.[21]

So if you decide college is not for you, what can you do instead?

Get a Job

If you decide you're not going to go to college, you can start working on your career right after graduation. Many people who finish their formal education with a high school diploma have successful careers and do fine financially. Believe it or not, Steve Jobs, the founder of Apple Computer, tried college for six months and dropped out. In a college commencement speech he gave in June 2005, he shared this story:

> After six months [in college], I couldn't see the value in it. I had no idea what I wanted to do with my life and no idea how college was going to help me figure it out. And here I was spending all of the money my parents had saved their entire life. So I decided to drop out and trust that it would all work out OK. It was pretty scary at the time, but looking back it was one of the best decisions I ever made. The minute I dropped out I could stop taking the required classes that didn't interest me, and begin dropping in on the ones that looked interesting.[22]

According to the website Business Insider, many well-paying jobs are open to people with a high school diploma. These jobs are in a variety of fields, including transportation, agriculture, communications, aviation, and more. Some may require a license or training, but they don't require a college degree. To find information about jobs that require just a high school diploma, visit the *Occupational Outlook Handbook* website (www.bls.gov/ooh). You

"Looking back it was one of the best decisions I ever made. The minute I dropped out [of college] I could stop taking the required classes that didn't interest me, and begin dropping in on the ones that looked interesting."[22]

—Steve Jobs, founder of Apple Computer

can search for jobs by the level of education required; choose "high school diploma or equivalent" to find jobs to consider.

While you may not need a degree for some jobs, that doesn't mean you can walk off the graduation stage and into a workplace and demand a high-paying job. As with any career, you need to be willing to start at the bottom and work your way up. You need to prove that you are a good, reliable worker eager and willing to learn. You need to make a commitment and know success will take time.

Students do not have to wait to graduate high school before they can learn job-related skills. Some high schools offer class-

Proficient computer skills can open doors for many positions. Many classes are available nights and weekends locally for those that work full-time.

Making a Budget

You need to be able to support yourself. Even if you live at home in your parents' basement, you'll need to make money. You can save it for the future, contribute to the bills, or spend it on your own needs and wants. If you live in your own place, then you definitely need money to pay the bills! Either way, now is a good time to get in the habit of making a budget.

A budget is a list of the money you have coming in (income) and a list of the money going out (expenses). Ideally, your income is more than your expenses. Your expenses will depend on where you're living. In addition, if you have a car, you need to pay for gas, insurance, and upkeep. If you use public transportation, you need to keep track of that, too. It's also a good idea to try to save a little money each month, if possible.

You may have to think about health insurance, too. Health insurance helps you pay for medical care if you get sick or injured. According to law, your parents can keep you on their health insurance until you turn twenty-six years old. If you cannot be on their insurance, it's a good idea to find your own and add that cost to your budget.

If you have access to the internet, you can search for information about making a budget and find sample budget forms.

es that teach coding, computer programming, marketing, child care, and more. Having this knowledge and/or skills to put on a job application or résumé can put job seekers ahead of other candidates.

Mike, who did not attend college after high school, took some vocational classes while in high school. He also took a photography class. As soon as his guidance counselor starting talking college, though, Mike tuned out. He was ready to put school behind him. After graduation, Mike started to play around more with his camera. He liked visiting run-down areas of his city to take pictures of dilapidated buildings and the people who lived around them. Then, when there were protests against racial inequalities in his city, he grabbed his camera, headed down to the action, and snapped pictures. He submitted some of his raw and emotional images to local newspapers, and one was accepted. Today Mike is working a part-time job to support himself, and he's spending the rest of his time taking pictures. He's selling more and more of them. No, he's not making a lot of money. But he's doing something he loves, and he's making a difference with his art.

Finding a Job After Graduation

Perhaps you're already working part-time after school and/or over summers. If so, is it a job you enjoy and can continue to do after graduation? If it is, maybe you could move up to make more money. Or perhaps you could keep the job as you look for a job that will lead to the career you have been considering. Either way, the skills you gain by working will help you as you work toward a career and even when you land the job you really want. Those skills include being on time for work, handling responsibilities, and working with coworkers, supervisors, and maybe the public. These are skills that only come with experience. They can't be taught at school. And employers are always looking for people who simply know how to have a job and go to work.

Tim, who now co-owns two successful restaurants, started as a waiter at a restaurant owned by his now business partner. At the time, Tim had not gone to college, but he worked hard and was dedicated to his job. His work ethic impressed the owner of the restaurant, who quickly promoted him. Tim worked his way up, saved money, and was asked to partner with his boss on a new restaurant. Tim's boss was his mentor; he showed him the ropes and helped him become a successful restaurant owner and effective boss. These were lessons Tim could not learn at college. "He believed in me and trusted me at an early age and taught me a lot about the business we are in,"[23] Tim said in a St. Louis magazine article in 2019. Eventually Tim did get an associate's degree to sharpen his business skills.

The Job Search

If you don't have a job or are ready to move on from your high school job, you'll need to begin a job search. That means filling out applications and going on interviews. The process is the same no matter when you look, no matter what kind of diploma or degree you have. Most job searches take place on the internet nowadays.

In addition to filling out applications, you might need a résumé too. It's a good idea to have one ready. Find books or websites

Having a complete résumé will help you to fill out job applications on site. It has all of your information at your fingertips.

to help you put one together. You can often find good samples online and use them to create your own. Have adults you trust look at your résumé to help ensure it's error-free.

The internet is your best bet for finding job openings. There are websites such as Indeed and Monster that will send jobs directly to your inbox. Go to their sites and search for the type of job you're looking for. Typically, the site will ask for a job title and a location. If you're looking for a job at a retail store, for example, type in "retail" and a drop-down menu will appear with different job titles. Choose one and then enter the location where you're

The Gig Economy

You may have heard the term *gig economy*, since it's pretty trendy right now. Simply put, gig work is what part-time workers or freelancers do. These are the people who drive a car for Uber, write or proofread magazine articles, or deliver your pizza. The people who do gig work say they are looking for a better balance between their work life and home life. Gig work allows them to make some money while still having flexibility to focus on other things.

Gig work has grown in popularity because technology such as Skype, Zoom, Slack, and Dropbox make working from just about anywhere possible. Gig workers can spend the day working on their passion for art, for example, and do gig work at night. It's a great way to make money while growing a side business, too. What's more, if you're new to the workforce, it's a good way to get your foot in the door at a company you might want to work for full-time someday.

There are some drawbacks to being a gig worker, however. Such jobs often come with no benefits such as vacation time or health insurance. Freelance work can be unpredictable—you never know when you might get work. And you need to have a lot self-discipline. It will be up to you alone to finish each project in the time alloted, as you won't have a boss looking over your shoulder.

looking to work. Click on the different jobs that come up to find the job description, qualifications, information about applying, and so on.

Applying for Jobs

When you find a job you want to apply for, you may be prompted to fill out an application. Most applications will request the same information, so have a list of the answers on your computer so you can cut and paste instead of retyping them over and over. If you fill out an application in person, bring a printout or handwritten list of this information with you so you can refer to it. Include a list of past jobs, with the dates you started and left, and the names of supervisors and their contact information. You'll also want to list your education history, including school names and dates of attendance and whether you graduated. Some companies may ask for your résumé and a cover letter, too. Read the job description and list of requirements for the job. Then tailor your résumé and cover letter to match. Again, search the internet or books for samples to help get you started.

The next step will be interviews. You may be asked a few questions over the phone, and if that goes well, the employer will ask you to come in for an in-person interview. Your appearance will matter, so be sure to wear appropriate clothes, look confident, make eye contact, and speak clearly. Even if you don't have all the qualifications or experience they're looking for, if you come off as a reliable, professional, likable person, chances are good you still will be considered for a job. For many jobs, skills can be taught. Character, on the other hand, is something that comes from within.

Starting Your Own Business

Many people know they don't want to work for someone else. They want to be their own boss. Or they know they have a great idea for a business, or they are very talented and hope to sell their creations. Starting a business is another option for the person with a high school diploma, but it's not an easy one. It can cost a lot of money, and you need to have some confidence that there are enough people out there who want the product or service you're selling.

At your age, the best way to start your own business is to start small. Get a part-time or full-time job and work on your business idea during your time off. For example, if you like to knit or sew, perhaps you could work on your craft in the evenings and on weekends. Once you have enough to sell, you could apply to sell your wares at local craft or art shows or farmers' markets. You also may be able to sell your work online through a marketplace such as Etsy.

Amanda took screenprinting and other art classes during and after high school. She perfected her art over time, putting her original designs on dishtowels and napkins. She sold her wares at small craft shows. In time and after a lot of work, local stores, and then national companies, wanted to sell her towels and napkins, too. Amanda earned enough money to buy her own equipment and today works out of her garage. She sells thousands of towels and napkins each year. "I wasn't ready for college after high school," Amanda says. "Then I found this hobby I really enjoyed. I feel so fortunate that I was able to turn a hobby I love into a career. I always encourage people to follow their heart in choosing a career. You will be much happier in the long run."[24]

If owning your own business appeals to you, it's never too early to start learning and preparing. Read books and search the internet for information about starting a business. Community colleges offer classes in how to run a business. Classes are a great

> "I always encourage people to follow their heart in choosing a career. You will be much happier in the long run."[24]
>
> —Amanda, business owner

way to learn and network with people who can give you advice about business ownership.

Getting a college degree is clearly not the only way to success. If you are unsure about or not ready to go to college, or you have no idea what you would study, don't spend money to figure it out. If you decide later you need or want a degree, then you can find a suitable program. Sometimes, getting some real-life experience may be just what you need to help you figure out "what you want to be when you grow up."

Chapter Five

Taking a Break

In many parts of Europe, most students who graduate from the equivalent of a US high school participate in what is known as a gap year. This is a year in which students travel, take an internship, and try to find out more about their place in the world. In the United States, however, a gap year traditionally has been seen as foolish, delaying, and self-indulgent. Yet a growing number of students are seeing the benefit of taking a break to think about their future before actively moving forward.

The Gap Year Option

In May 2012 Maria Shriver, a well-known journalist and writer, gave a commencement speech at the Annenberg School for Communications and Journalism at the University of Southern California, where her daughter Katherine Schwarzenegger was graduating. She was speaking to college graduates, but her words ring equally true for high school graduates: "Before you go out and press that Fast Forward button, I'm hoping—I'm praying—that you'll have the courage to first press the Pause button. . . . Pausing allows you to take a beat—to take a breath in your life."[25]

When Schwarzenegger shared her mother's words in her book, *I Just Graduated, Now What?*, she asked her to explain what she meant by "pausing." Shriver said: "It's really important to pause along the way and take a break from communicating outwardly, so you can communicate inwardly, with yourself. PAUSE—and take the time to find out what's important to you. Find out what you love, what's real and true to you—so it can infuse and inform your work and make it your own. . . . . It's okay not to know what you're going to do!"[26]

Shriver's advice can apply to high school graduates. And even after college graduation, a person still may not know what to do next. Taking a pause can help you figure out what is the next best step.

Gap Year Association, a nonprofit organization that helps young adults who want to take a break after high school to volunteer in other countries, defines a gap year as "a semester or year of experiential learning, typically taken after high school and prior to career or post-secondary education, in order to deepen one's practical, professional, and personal awareness."[27]

The gap year can be the defining year to help you move forward with life plans.

"A gap year is a wonderful opportunity for young people to take a year to follow a passion before attending college."[28]

—Avis Hinkson, dean of Barnard College in New York

According to Avis Hinkson, dean of Barnard College in New York, "A gap year is a wonderful opportunity for young people to take a year to follow a passion before attending college. Some will have internships, some will travel, some will fulfill religious responsibilities and some find paid work. All-in-all they will grow and mature."[28]

Gap Year Association estimates that each year 30,000 to 40,000 U.S. students take a gap year. The idea is that after some time off, a student will head to college with a clearer head and a better idea of what to do next. Today, students spend their gap years in several ways. Here some examples:

- Volunteer either close to home or in another country. Different groups organize volunteer opportunities in other countries. Check out Aardvark Israel, Art History Abroad, and Gap Year Association. Your guidance counselor also can help you find information or steer you in the right direction.

- Travel and experience a different culture. Some people travel to simply explore the world and other cultures. There isn't always a volunteer element to it. Some companies offer organized group travel, such as Amigo International, Where There Be Dragons, and Thinking Beyond Borders. If travel abroad is not affordable or you'd rather not go far away, you can travel around the United States, too. Or you can even do virtual tours of places of interest, including museums.

- Take classes to learn skills or a new language. Classes "just for fun" can help you discover careers and vocations that you've never had time to explore. It can be a relief to take courses where it's the experience that matters, not the grades. Taking classes also keeps you in the learning mind-set.

- Get ready for college—mentally and emotionally. Some overstressed high school students simply need time to experience life without a lot of structure and activity. This can be a good time to take some classes in meditation or yoga. Some can be found online for free or a small fee.

- Work and save money. Whether you think you'll go to college or not, a gap year gives you time to increase your savings.

AmeriCorps

If you decide to take a gap year and want to do volunteer work, you might want to consider AmeriCorps. Not only will you volunteer your time to help others in need, but you will gain professional skills and an experience that will stay with you the rest of your life. AmeriCorps is a network of local, state, and national service organizations that connects more than seventy-five thousand Americans in service each year to meet community needs. According to its website, "members of AmeriCorps commit their time to address critical community needs like increasing academic achievement, mentoring youth, fighting poverty, sustaining national parks, preparing for disasters, and more."

People who sign up with AmeriCorps work in part- and full-time positions for three to twelve months. For full-time service, members receive up to $4,725 to pay for college or graduate school or to pay back qualified student loans. Part-time members receive a partial award. Members also have access to other benefits such as health insurance. Within AmeriCorps, there are three different programs, each with a different focus.

To join AmeriCorps, you must be at least seventeen years old, be a US citizen, have a high school diploma (or be willing to work toward one), and be able to commit to at least one year of service. For more information about AmeriCorps, visit its website at www.nationalservice.gov/programs/americorps.

AmeriCorps, "AmeriCorps." www.nationalservice.gov.

Gap Year Benefits

A gap year can be a good idea for many reasons. Think about it: you've been going to school your whole life. Some time off from the structure of classrooms, computers, textbooks, and homework can be good for the mind, body, and soul. If you're not sure what to do after graduation, a gap year can give you time to stop and explore what you really want to do next.

Volunteering with an organization of your choice can be a rewarding experience.

Deferring a College Acceptance

If you've been accepted to a college but want to take a year off before beginning classes, there's a chance you can. With deferred enrollment, you can request the college hold your spot for up to a year. It's important, however, that you find out what the deferment will mean for any financial aid the school has offered. You may have to reapply for the aid, and you may or may not get the same offer. Before the school agrees to let you skip a year, it may want to know more about your reasons for wanting to delay your attendance and what you plan to do with the extra time. The chances that the college will agree to let you delay the start of your freshman year will be greater if you follow their instructions for making the request.

Here are general guidelines for deferring enrollment:

- Send a letter to the college's office of admissions to let the school know you want to take a gap year and why. Send this letter no later than June of the year you plan to defer.

- The admissions office will confirm or deny your request. If you receive a denial, you will have choices to make. However, if the school accepted you once, chances are it will again. If taking a gap year is truly what you want to do, it may be worth the risk.

In a *New York Times* article, Abby Falik, founder and chief executive officer of Global Citizen Year, an organization that runs a gap year fellowship, says that "graduating seniors see this time not as a derailment of plans, but as a 'purpose year' that can ground them, challenge them and make them better students later on."[29] Some people think that when a student takes a gap year, he or she will never go back to school. That doesn't appear to be the case. According to the Gap Year Association, "90 percent of students go on to enroll in a four-year institution within one year of completing their gap year."[30] And studies have shown that taking a gap year can increase success in college and is related to job satisfaction later in life.

Of course, for some a gap *year* becomes gap *years*. And there is nothing wrong with that, as long as they're doing something that makes them happy and gives them a sense of purpose.

Making a Plan

If you're considering taking a year off, it's a good idea to have a plan. Make a list of the things you'd like to accomplish. Set goals and share them with friends and adults you trust. Sharing goals helps keep you accountable. A year can go by quickly, so check in with yourself once a month or so to see whether you're sticking to your goals. If not, you may want to make some adjustments.

The bottom line is that there is no one way to do life after high school. For years, many students have followed the same path, going to college and getting a job. There are so many more options now, and so many reasons to think long and hard about taking the usual route. Some people, like Christy, now a teacher, look back on their lives after high school and wish they'd done things differently: "There is so much to life after high school—I know that is so cliché to say, but it is what I have found to be true. I honestly wish I had more skills around home improvement (plumbing, electrical, and so on). Figure out what type of life will make you happy and go for it—don't let people bring you down along the way. If you have faith in yourself, use

"There is so much to life after high school. . . . I honestly wish I had more skills around home improvement (plumbing, electrical, and so on). Figure out what type of life will make you happy and go for it—don't let people bring you down along the way. If you have faith in yourself, use all available resources that are there to support your decision, and stay the course even when it is really hard."[31]

—Christy, teacher

all available resources that are there to support your decision, and stay the course even when it is really hard."[31]

Going to college right after high school is still a great choice for many students, and college can lead you on a path to great things. But it's perfectly normal and okay if you don't know what you want to do or if you want to do something that no one expects. As with any big decision in your life, it's important to discuss your choices with people around you whom you trust, love, and respect. Those people will support you no matter what you decide to do, and they will give you honest advice.

Conclusion

Whether you're a freshman or senior, high school graduation will be here before you know it. No matter what your year, it's never too early or too late to start thinking and planning what you will do once you walk off that stage with your diploma. The options for high school graduates are greater and more varied than ever. And for most people, the stigma of not going to college is no longer a factor. It is common knowledge now that college can be incredibly expensive, and more and more college graduates walk out of college with a degree in one hand and a large amount of debt in the other. Regardless of what anyone thinks—from your high school friends to your grandparents to your teachers and counselors—what you do after college is a decision you need to make for yourself. Yes, you want advice from those whom you know and who love you best, but in the end, you need to live with the decision. Whether you decide to take a gap year or forgo college altogether is all up to you.

Brooke, a college graduate who is now a marketing manager, advises:

> Take it seriously to set yourself up for success, but also remember to have fun. . . . You want to accomplish things that you're proud of while also enjoying the ride. Find someone older who's successful professionally (and/or personally!) in a way you'd like to be and get advice from them. Don't make huge life-altering decisions completely on your own; talk to a mentor to get some other perspectives before you make your big life decisions.[32]

Making big decisions is not easy, no matter how old you are or how much experience you have. Choosing a path to your future can be overwhelming and anxiety producing, for sure. But it can also be fun, exciting, and exhilarating, especially if you take a deep breath and use the resources available to you. You have people around you who can provide help, such as information, assistance with research, and advice. Plus, you have the internet to help you navigate. Colleges, volunteer organizations, trade schools, and more all have websites to get you started. No calling strangers or figuring out what to ask. Most of what you need is right there in the drop-down menus and search bars.

"Take it seriously to set yourself up for success, but also remember to have fun. . . . You want to accomplish things that you're proud of while also enjoying the ride. Find someone older who's successful professionally (and/or personally!) in a way you'd like to be and get advice from them. Don't make huge life-altering decisions completely on your own; talk to a mentor to get some other perspectives before you make your big life decisions."[32]

—Brooke, marketing manager

This is an exciting and possibly nerve-wracking time in your life. You are at a time when you must look ahead and choose the path to your future. It can also be overwhelming and confusing. This is why you need to keep in mind that whatever you decide for yourself now, you have plenty of time to change course along the way. If you find months or years later that your decision wasn't quite right or you'd like to try something new, that's perfectly okay. You can pack up what you learned and your experiences and use your resources to forge another path.

Just know that there is no one path to success in life. Everyone make mistakes, and everyone is allowed do-overs. You may think this can't possibly be true. Go ahead and ask people who've been in your shoes what they would have done differently, and you will get an earful of answers and advice. Very few people feel they got everything exactly right as they worked toward their career. But this is what makes life interesting—you never really know for sure where you'll end up until you get there. And once you're there, you might want to move on to the next place. Gabe, a college-bound student, says:

> People tend to want things to be absolutely perfect and take just the right path, but that's not how things work. I wouldn't be who I was if I didn't make the failures that I did. Would I have studied more for one quiz to get my GPA higher so I looked better on applications? Duh, who wouldn't? But preparing for college is about more than just what you look like on a piece of paper.[33]

Your future is ahead; plan, prepare, and go for it.

Madi, a graphic designer, has this advice: "Don't be afraid to follow an untraditional path. Do what's right for you, not what you feel you *should* do."[34] What's truly important is that you find a career that you love, one that you are passionate about. Your life's work need not be just about making money. It should make you happy. It should make you proud. You should look forward to doing your work each day. Not everyone achieves this level of job satisfaction, but it's definitely a worthy goal. And if you start thinking and planning your future now, it's a lot more likely that you'll reach that goal.

"Don't be afraid to follow an untraditional path. Do what's right for you, not what you feel you *should* do."[34]

—Madi, graphic designer

Source Notes

Chapter One: Eyeing the Future

1. CareerShip, "About CareerShip." http://mappingyour future.org.
2. Gabe, interview with the author, June 2, 2020.
3. Emily, interview with the author, June 2, 2020.
4. Quoted in Brainy Quote, "Stephen Colbert Quotes," 2020. www.brainyquote.com.
5. Carl, interview with the author, April 7, 2020.
6. Christy, interview with the author, April 5, 2020.

Chapter Two: College Bound

7. Katherine Schwarzenegger, *I Just Graduated . . . Now What?* New York: Crown Archetype, 2014, pp. 1–2.
8. Education USA, "Community College." https://educa tionusa.state.gov.
9. Chad Orzel, "Four Important Things to Consider When Choosing a College," *Forbes*, February 19, 2016. www .forbes.com.
10. Sophie, interview with the author, June 6, 2020.
11. Navid, interview with the author, April 2, 2020.
12. Emily, interview with the author, June 2, 2020.
13. Myla, interview with the author, June 5, 2020.
14. Sera, interview with the author, April 2, 2020.
15. Riley, interview with the author, June 2, 2020.
16. Quoted in Kelly Mae Ross, "A Complete Guide to the College Application Process," *U.S. News & World Report*, March 8, 2018. www.usnews.com.
17. Madi, interview with the author, April 2, 2020.

Chapter Three: Alternatives to Traditional College

18. Lia, interview with the author, April 3, 2020.

19. Bill, interview with the author, April 3, 2020.
20. Matthew Crawford, "The Case for Working with Your Hands," *New York Times Magazine*, May 21, 2009. www.nytimes.com.

Chapter Four: Careers Without College
21. Quoted in Schwarzenegger, *I Just Graduated . . . Now What?*, p. 65.
22. Steve Jobs, "I'm Glad I Dropped Out of College," LewRockwell.com. August 26, 2011. www.lewrockwell.com.
23. *St. Louis (MO) Business Journal*, "30 Under 30: 2019, Tim Wiggins, on Point Hospitality." July 12, 2019. www.bizjournals.com.
24. Amanda, interview with the author, July 9, 2020.

Chapter Five: Taking a Break
25. Quoted in Schwarzenegger, *I Just Graduated . . . Now What?*, p. 5.
26. Quoted in Schwarzenegger, *I Just Graduated . . . Now What?*, p. 7.
27. Gap Year Association, "What Is a Gap Year?," 2020. www.gapyearassociation.org.
28. Quoted in Jessica Dickler, "Making the Most of a Gap Year Before College," CNBC, May 19, 2017. www.cnbc.com.
29. Quoted in Melody Warnick, "Gap Year Ideas for College Students," *New York Times*, April 23, 2020. www.nytimes.com.
30. Gap Year Association, "What Is a Gap Year?"
31. Christy, interview with the author, April 3, 2020.

Conclusion
32. Brooke, interview with the author, April 2, 2020.
33. Gabe, interview with the author, June 2, 2020.
34. Madi, interview with the author.

Books

Carol Christen and Richard Bowles, *What Color Is Your Parachute for Teens: Discover Yourself Design Your Future, and Plan for Your Dream Job*. New York: Ten Speed, 2015.

Anna Costaras and Gail Liss, *The College Bound Organizer: The Ultimate Guide to Successful College Applications*. Coral Gables, FL: Mango, 2018.

Ryan Craig and Allen Blue, *A New U: Faster and Cheaper Alternatives to College*. Dallas, TX: Ben Bella Books, 2018.

Edward Fiske, *Fiske Guide to Colleges 2020*. Naperville, IL: Soucebooks, 2019.

Gen Tanabe and Kelly Tanabe, *The Ultimate Scholarship Book 2020: Billions of Dollars in Scholarships, Grants and Prizes.* Belmont, CA: SuperCollege, 2019.

Paul Tieger, Barbara Barron, and Kelly Tieger, *Do What You Are: Discover the Perfect Career for You Through the Secrets of Personality Type.* New York: Little, Brown, 2014.

Yale Daily News Staff, *The Insider's Guide to Colleges: Students on Campus Tell You What You Really Want to Know*. New Haven, CT: Yale Daily News, 2015.

Internet Sources

AmeriCorps, "AmeriCorps." www.nationalservice.gov.

Matthew Crawford, "The Case for Working with Your Hands," *New York Times Magazine*, May 21, 2009. www.nytimes.com.

Katie Creel, "What Is College Today?," Colleges of Distinction, 2020. https://collegesofdistinction.com.

Jessica Dickler, "Making the Most of a Gap Year Before College," CNBC, May 19, 2017. www.cnbc.com.

Education USA, "Community College." https://educationusa .state.gov.

Kate Evans, "Why and How to Defer College Acceptance for a Gap Year," Go Overseas, May 26, 2020. www.gooverseas.com.

Robert Farrington, "Here's Every Reason You Should Take a Gap Year Before College," *Forbes*, June 10, 2019. www.forbes.com.

Gap Year Association, "What Is a Gap Year?," 2020. www.gap yearassociation.org.

Fiona Hollands and Aasiya Kazi, "MOOC-Based Alternative Credentials: What's the Value for the Learner?," *Educause Review*, June 3, 2019. https://er.educause.edu.

Chad Orzel, "Four Important Things to Consider When Choosing a College," *Forbes*, February 19, 2016. www.forbes.com.

Cheryl Preheim and Donesha Aldridge, "Georgia High School Senior Receives 32 College Acceptance Letters, $500K in Scholarship Offers," KSDK.com, May 13, 2020. www.ksdk.com.

Cheryl Preheim and Christopher Buchanan, "Georgia Teen Accepted to 31 Schools Goes Viral for Inspiring Photo," KSDK.com, February 27, 2019. www.ksdk.com.

Kelly Mae Ross, "College vs. University in the U.S.: What's the Difference?," *U.S. News & World Report*, July 6, 2018. www.us news.com.

Kelly Mae Ross, "A Complete Guide to the College Application Process," *U.S. News & World Report*, March 8, 2018. www.us news.com.

Michelle Singletary, "Is College Still Worth It? Read This Study," *Washington Post*, January 11, 2020. www.washingtonpost.com.

Elka Torpey, "Measuring the Value of an Education," Bureau of Labor Statistics, April 2018. www.bls.gov.

Volunteer Florida, "How to Join AmeriCorps," 2020. www.volunteerflorida.org.

Melody Warnick, "Gap Year Ideas for College Students," *New York Times*, April 23, 2020. www.nytimes.com.

Whitney Blair Wyckoff, "The 25 Best Jobs of 2020," *U.S. News & World Report*, January 7, 2020. https://money.usnews.com.

Websites

Bureau of Labor Statistics (www.bls.gov). This comprehensive government website is a great resource to learn about careers, including salary, education requirements, outlook, and more.

CareerShip (http://mappingyourfuture.org). Students can use this website to explore careers and prepare for college, including finding scholarships and other financial aid.

College Confidential (www.collegeconfidential.com). On this college forum, you can search schools and find out more about their admission requirements, student body, and more.

Colleges That Change Lives (CTCL.org). This nonprofit organization is dedicated to helping each and every student find a college that develops a lifelong love of learning. This website introduces users to colleges and universities that have a student-centered focus.

Education Conservancy (www.educationconservancy.org). This is a nonprofit organization committed to improving college admission processes for students, colleges, and high schools.

Enrichment Alley (www.enrichmentalley.com). A database of summer programs for high school students and others. The site allows users to search using criteria that are important to them. You can hunt for summer programs by subject, location, and type, such as academic, community service, internship, or travel opportunity.

Gap Year Association (www.gapyearassociation.org). This website helps students understand what a gap year is and explore their options to make the best of taking a year off before attending college.

Index

Picture Credits

About the Author

Katie John Sharp graduated from high school in three years and immediately went to college thinking she wanted to be a preschool teacher. Once in college, she changed her mind several times and graduated with a degree in community health education. Now she's living in St. Louis, Missouri, and working as a freelance writer and editor. She's proof positive that career paths continue to meander throughout our lives.